101 Lentos

Poems of the New Millennium
Featuring Poets Across the World

notionpress.com

101 Lentos

Poems of the New Millennium
Featuring Poets Across the World

Lencio Rodrigues

notionpress.com

Notion Press

5 Muthu Kalathy Street, Triplicane,

Chennai - 600 005

First Published by Notion Press 2013

ISBN: 978-93-83416-45-5

For My Parents
Sebastião Luis Rodrigues & Filomena Pinto

Acknowledgement

My sincere thanks to all the wonderful writers in this book for their contribution, support and friendship.

Prologue

Everything in our world moves with time. It is the apparent trend we call "change", one that we all require to shed the boredom and live through the day. Tradition can be mind-numbing and as human history goes, someone somewhere strives to make a change. We all dream of a change and look forward to an invention.

It was in one such dream; the idea of the Lento crossed the backroom of my mind. I knew, and so well aware of the mixed reactions of such a modification to this ancient tradition. Nevertheless if poetry is a way of getting your innermost thoughts across, how you write it, doesn't really matter. Or does it?

Today, I am happy the Lento is well received by poets across the world, who find it challenging, novel and fun! This book showcases some of the most extraordinary poets of our time. These are people from all walks of life, ranging from ages 15 to 85, and from all over the world, some, whose primary language is not English, but like you and me, revere literature and seek therapy through poetry. Varying significantly in subject, each poet offers a feast to the senses through these splendid Lentos.

101 Lentos has been an amazing and fulfilling journey meeting these wonderful people across the globe whose vision has been similar yet the rendering, limitless. It has been both fun and frustrating, but as a farmer of a plenteous harvest rejoices, I am more than ecstatic to see this fruit ripen. Only what saddens me right now, are those few who couldn't make it to the peak of this adventurous voyage. May their souls rest in peace and may God give their families the comfort for their loss.

The Top Three Golden Trophy Winners

Featuring in this book are Lentos that are mainly selected for their unreservedly refreshing ideas and themes. Many poets have been invited to write exclusively for this book. Several contests were also conducted to decide on the best pieces. Here are three of the many winners that have won these contests.

A Thief in the Night

B. Hopkins
West Midlands, United Kingdom

To reap the beggar's life, untouched by gold;
through fate or chance? I do not understand,
you tell me humbly bow, accept what is,
eschew I will, the pauper's empty hand.

Thief, they call me now, what care have I?
Belief they have that bids them curse me so;
lief, I stalk the night, a shadow's dark
grief is all my purpose shall bestow.

Scorn, I must, this conscience, foolish grained
born was I, to taste the manna, greed;
forewarn you may the lamb this wolf can see
mourn they will, as long, this wolf shall feed.

My coffers now are bulging, satisfied
goodbye, I snarl at baneful poverty;
why should I regret my chosen path?
die I will, this life, in luxury.

SUMMER SASSAFRAS

Mark Andrew James Terry
Orlando, Florida, USA

Grass is floating with the wind,
bass are treading, feathers spreading,
mass in movement, all chagrinned
Sassafras is shedding.

Tea refined by bark and leaves,
auxiliary perfumery.
See the tree and how it grieves
the heat's infirmary.

The Lost Bullocky

David P. Wilkins
Annandale, NSW, Australia

Yoked in pairs, eight bullocks pulled the dray.
Soaked by fear, the driver steered his team.
Cloaked in dust and drought he stopped to pray,
choked back tears and asked to be redeemed.

Men out hunting heard the bullock bells.
Ten hot days, the dray was off its track,
when, half-dead, the bullocky heard yells,
then, by Grace, the hunters brought him back.

A Country Road at Night

Stephen A. Carter
Port Coquitlam, Vancouver, BC, Canada.

Ted and I drove along a country road at night.
Dead ahead he tried to swerve around a bear that
Fled out of forest shadows into moonlight.
Headlights froze the poor beast in an instant.

We saw it smash into the right side of the car.
Free of the impact we stopped and climbed out.
"See!" Ted cried, "We scared if off afar."
He was wrong. I didn't have time to shout.

A Lento Song

Agatha Lai
Kudat, Malaysia

Angels, once you stood beside my bed;
bubbles of faith dwindle as I grow tall.
Troubles, when you step in odors spread;
battles torment men between wall and wall.

Mother, pillar of our home, you spin and toil;
feather pillows you made cushion my head.
Brother, go and plant seeds on tilled ground;
gather ripen grains to fill the wooden shed.

Hail peace, shun war, beg the earth not to quake.
Trail Eden Park to ease the heated mind.
Sail to where pale lilies sway in the breeze.
Veil surly thoughts; let's leave the din behind.

Stray along the edges of shady paths.
Away, see how profusely daisies spread.
Survey cute things at stores, relish plain food;
delay returning home till sun is red.

A Matter of Debate

M. P. Myers
Tucson, Arizona, USA

It starts in autumn after one brief lull.
Wit and wisdom will not suffice.
Mitt is out of touch, Barack is not dull.
Sit right down...I'll give you advice!

Come shuffle the cards to see who's lyin';
Hum "Eeny, meeny, miny, moe."
From Biden's touchin' to sharp-tongued Ryan,
some say, "Just keep the status quo".

A Mother's Commitment

By Victoria Sutton
Texas, USA

Believe! All dreams are filled by hands of another
Receive the love that motherly bosoms maintain;
retrieve those bad thoughts before words are spun!
Deceive not the life who's given birth, from anger abstain.

Pursue the moments to come, the future with child
Two hearts, two souls forever entwining;
You and I, mother, daughter, fulfilling our dreams.
Who would have guessed, you'd be my brightest star shining?

Trust me when I say, " I love you. Always & Forever."
Must I repeat it? Or do you understand?
Rust comes from idle settling. Pursue, achieve, and be proud.
Just know that no matter what, by you, I will forever stand.

Around my neck a golden locket is worn
Found in it a picture of your precious smile
Sound of your laughter is carried in the wind
Profound is the presence that lingers awhile.

A Reminder

Khalid M. Darwish
Damascus, Syria

Man, only you choose the right way for your life
when your wrong ways appear to be crowded
Tens of thousands only succeed in their strife
Then they expect someday to be shrouded

We don't ask for a world of no murders
certainly though, of no justification to kill
Be in life like strangers or wayfarers
Humbly cut the rope of cheating and lies you spill

A Sinner Repents

John Peter Creighton
Oak Wood Hills, Illinois, USA

Now in this moment I'm in the second day,
Allow me to say, of the newest stage of my recovery.
However you see this phenomenon, for mè it's immediate
Ow! and yet so far away, desired discovery.

You seem to think it's easy to be me,
to do the things and feel the feelings you don't know.
A Jew, Muslim, Christian, Buddhist all contend,
whoever too, among us human though.

Nard of incense slowly scented incense burning.
Card was dealt: young fools loving.
Ardent lovers can't stand waiting.
Bards sang and joked while angels hovering.

Shards were healed by men in brothering.
Guards need to stand then take a break.
Hard can be for drunk recovery.
Dart might pierce so truth can take.

Airport Goodbyes

June Collini
Melbourne, Australia

Crying as I hug and kiss the people I hold dear
Drying my eyes in an attempt to hide the pain
Trying to be brave as the time to leave draws near
Sighing as I wonder when we all will meet again

Delaying and searching for the last few words to say
Betraying my feelings as more tears well in my eyes
Praying for safe journeys as I watch them walk away
Displaying all the agony of airport goodbyes

Almighty, My Treasure Trove

Sukmawati Komala
Jakarta, Indonesia

Kill my pride with your healing vision
Fill me Lord with your softest love
Till your words charge life into me
Will worship Almighty, my treasure trove

Continuous praises to your supreme presence
Joyous worship to delight your holy heart
Courageous spirits declare your graceful glory
Gracious blessings bestowed from heaven's cart

Amor's Chalice

Ingrid de Klerck
Voorburg, The Netherlands

Thinking about you sets my heart ablaze,
drinking from Amor's chalice once again,
linking our destinies in silent praise.
Winking at us: life's sweetest champagne.

Teach me, show me love in all its splendor,
reach for the ultimate sexual fantasy.
Preach to me about complete surrender,
each day celebrated in blissful ecstasy.

Apocalypse

Sharyn Stone
Huelo, Maui, Hawaii

I who built this earth in glory
cry at seeing you succumb,
Why have you abused my riches?
Fie on all that you've become!

Do not war on my Creation
You incur my wrath times ten,
Who mistreats my world of wonders?
Rue this day, you world of men!

Blow, my winds and racing clouds now
Throw my spears of fury's rain
Lo, the sounds of thunder roaring
Flow wild cataracts again!

Brawl, my ocean's crazing waters
Crawl, all creatures, hide you well,
Wall of waves roll now to drown you
All is ending - toll death's knell!

Ashes to Ashes

Wendy R. Blair
Roanoke, Virginia, USA

Haunted by her father's death.
Vaunted child, to servant's role.
Taunted with their every breath.
Flaunted wealth, her home they stole.

Scrubs the chimney sweeps the ash.
Rubs the silver makes it glow.
Grubs for supper from their trash.
Stubs of candles gutter low.

Seeming to be meek and cowed.
Steaming with the insults hurled.
Scheming stepchild, plotting, proud.
Screaming self inside her, furled.

Sates their every whim, command.
Plaits their hair with fingers numb.
Hates each servile act's demand.
Waits for any fallen crumb.

Sashes for their lovely gowns.
Clashes over jewels and hair.
Lashes from their tongues and frowns.
Ashes for her heart to wear.

Sighing as she sweeps each grate,
Drying tears she can't allow.
Vying with her vicious fate,
Crying out she makes a vow.

"To the ball I'll find a way.
Through my wiles, a crown I'll catch.
Rue the day, for then you'll pay.
True love, ha! The prince my match"

Drew she blood spells from the ground.
Grew the pumpkin coach-and-four.
Through dark magic groomed and gowned,
Coup begun, revenge in store.

Fairy wrought glass slippers spun.
Tarry not, till midnight lent.
Marry him, there will be none
Wary of her true intent.

Wed to Prince, his kingdom shared.
Dead stepsisters, how, who knows?
Dread the fate of those who dared
Tread on Cinderella's toes.

Asylum

Erleen Alvarez
Camarines Norte, Philippines

Keeping my mind blank
Avoiding the haunting image
Thinking other things than
Killing myself in this cage

Insanity took the best of me
Fatality will cradle me to sleep
Misery will soon depart
Mortality is hard to keep

An Autumn Farewell

Janet Jongebloed
Lake Ronkonkoma, New York, USA

Trees line streets of fallen golden leaves,
Ease of summer days is far behind,
Freeze will be coming with the winter.
Please let the warmth return and rewind.

Balking at the changing of the days,
Walking through streets of soft fading light,
Hawking presents you once gave to me,
Stalking through the darkness of the night.

Missing the times that have gone before,
Kissing memories a sad goodbye,
Reminiscing brings only more pain.
Dismissing our love, I cry and sigh.

No one can stop the sad flow of life.
Snow comes like a banshee every year.
Though the season may return again...
Go my love - I shall wait for you here.

Balmoral Beach

David Williams
Southport, England, United Kingdom

Unfurling under a hot summer sun
Whirling tide pounding the beach
Curling up with a favourite book
Hurling bread to gulls, hear them screech.

Playing games, beach volley ball
Praying that the day would not end
Swaying, with each incoming wave
Straying to seclusion, with a lady friend!

Beyond

Marion Mantel
Vence, France

Between each thought, before each birth of breath,
unseen, a silent Presence wakes behind
the scene of ego-battles bound to death
and meaningless contortions of the mind.

Below the war of waves that crown the sea,
I know the Source of Stillness that's my core
bestowing blessings on each part of "me":
free flowing drop of Ocean without shore.

This Ocean that all drops long to embrace –
devotion as their only inner guide –
dwells motionless, transcending realms of space,
emotionally free from time and tide.

Its name is Peace, its nature vast and free;
the same as pure Awareness, Bliss, or Grace.
No frame can hold this Joy: to simply Be;
my flame thus swallowed, "I" shall leave no trace ...

Bleeding Roses

Josephine Vella
Central Coast, New South Wales, Australia

Bleeding roses never reveal their hurt
Pleading with themselves to carry on instead
Weeding out the negatives with protective thorns
Feeding their souls with tears once shed.

Learning from mistakes, made in their life
Yearning for a new start to every day
Burning with a desire to blush once more
Turning heads at their brilliant display.

Challenges of Life

Charishma Navneet Gupta
Muscat, Sultanate of Oman

When winds of change try to rock your boat
Then close your eyes, look within and pray,
Men of all kinds will cross your path on earth
Ten thousand times repeat His name in prayer.

He is benevolent, omnipresent and all-merciful
Free from boundaries of caste, creed and income,
Be in an attitude of gratitude towards the Master
See then your life as colourful as spring become.

Chances In Life

Ibrahim Dwidar
Cairo, Egypt

Light is shining from her eyes
Night is turning into dawn
Sight so beautiful, drawing me to her
Bright, my life as a sunny morn.

Thinking inside my heady head
Dreaming of first contact
Imagining me walking to her
Smiling of the ways to connect.

Attracted by her moves here, there,
Tracked by people everywhere
Crafted by her presence, awesome scenes
Thirsted, seeing nothing but her stunning stare.

Streams of ideas are blowing my head
Dreams may soon come true
Seems to me such moments must end
Beams or silent screams, wish I know...

Few steps and I can reach happiness
Truly hard but she's really worth it
Throughout eternity I shan't have a chance as this
True or untrue, will know that in just a bit.

Moving to the other side of the basement
Having nothing but my heart as guide
Coming to her with emotions like flames burning
Nothing wrong if I failed, at least I'll be happy I tried

Hi! nice weather, isn't it?
Sigh! was her only response to me
Why on earth is she looking at me like that!
Eyes so charming like a deep blue sea.

Would it be silly if we walked together?
"You'd never ask for this, I thought", she said with eyes of wit
Good you asked because if you didn't,
I could cross the street and ask for it.

Moment lost in fear is a chance lost forever
Torrent of pain following from reject
And if we miss some chances, we
spend all our lifetime in regret.

Better always to be an adventurer
Rather than staying safe in neglected part
Happier life comes only to a warrior
Loser of some battles will one day win the perfect heart!

Coping by Riding

Jenny Good
Texas, USA

Pounding hooves bounce off the canyon walls
Sounding like a derby at full speed
Rounding corners, praying for no falls
Bounding up the rocks on my swift steed

Riding takes me to a higher place
Gliding through the air as if I'm free
Siding with The source of light and grace
Biding to a truer part of me

Flying out across the prairie sky
Trying out the wings around my heart
Crying over all the years gone by
Drying tears to make a brand new start

Coping with my grief in such a way
Hoping that these rides will never cease
Roping all that's good from each new day
Loping into future promised peace

County Fair

Ken Johnson
Locust Grove, Virginia, USA

Bright colors waving in the air
delight the waiting children's eyes,
incite imagination's flair,
invite the sound of joyful cries.

Files of gawkers fill the park;
trials of skill and strength abound.
Miles of walking until dark;
aisles of mirrors to confound.

Corn freshly popped, apples of red,
adorn the midway's gaudy stands;
warn of stomach aches ahead
borne on sticky little hands.

Replete with every game of chance,
deceit shines in the hawker's eyes.
"Beat me," he says with just a glance -
defeat comes as no surprise.

Sheep and cows and pies and bread
reap the glory, ribbons bright.
Asleep, the toddlers nod their head,
deep in dreamland for the night.

Blue to black, the day is past,
debut the stars that now appear.
Hue and cry fades at long last.
Adieu until the fair next year!

Creole Country

Elise Lahr
Pennsylvania USA

Soon the sizzling sun will burst bright
Noon spearmint chilled ice tea, the scent of fresh cut blue grass
Moon hazy hovers over the lazy river
June rod baited, hooked and fishing for Bass

Sightsee in Creole country
Oak tree protecting from southern sun
Jamboree festivals, catfish jambalaya, along the Bayou
Honeybees buzz to Louisiana fun

Dancing Lights

Phyllis Babcock
Regina, Saskatchewan, Canada

Glow of lights dancing in the sky
Flow of movement in twilight
Grow visions of colorful hues
Throw star dust into the night.

Night prevails in magical glow
Height of perfection patterns appear
Lights radiant, reflect in the sky
Sight exquisite ~ our heaven's near.

Daybreak

Linda Rivas Bole
Conneautville, Pennsylvania, USA

day breaks on a beautiful autumn scene
stay where you are, watch the deer nibble a wild flower
play with the wind as it passes through your fingers
pray with the clouds that drift by the hour

night comes quickly in autumn's lovely grace
sight of so much color makes me feel bubbly inside
delight in the seasons is my forever amazement
bright colors wait for glorious mornings pride

Depictions

Sally Yocom
Columbus, Ohio, USA.

The arts are black within my man.
Assertively they storm.
He changes moods without a plan.
We can't predict their form.

Cold ice is he, like pictured stars,
Old light in photoed sky,
Controlled as Mercury or Mars,
Extolled by such as I.

Perhaps he's like an angry verse,
Scraps scrawled on wadded sheet,
Rattraps of words that cry and curse,
Relapse to vain conceit.

Or else he's like a painted ship
Offshore on canvas sea,
Wherefore his harsh, unmoving trip
More dark and still will be.

To me he's now a play on stage,
Untrue, a simple scene.
Through phrases written on a page,
Few feelings can I glean.

At times he's like a torso, hewn,
That sits upon a shelf,
Aristocrat, to love immune,
Begat of stone itself.

He's but a shape, a nice design,
These features painted on.
Seize life, I muse. It should be mine.
Ease out, withdraw, begone.

Why still does coldness heat my heart?
I close my eyes and cry.
My mind says leave this piece of art.
Goodbye, my love. Goodbye.

Despair

James Fraser
Inverness, Scotland

Bore after bore fell silent eventually
Abhor I do feel through my eyes
Gore and sore now abundantly plenty
Tore through clouds, wondrous skies

Despair in abundance appears all around
Where in the world has all our love gone
Stare into our abyss, and see it abound
There is no tomorrow, there is no dawn

Donna 'Dawn till Dusk'

Zelick Mendelovich
Leeds, United Kingdom

"*Banana I love you*" said Pumpkin the plump
Santana stood frozen a plum on his rump
Nanna said "*Yo! You ain't Forrest Gump*"
Branna, stand straight! I hate when you slump!

Nag in the morning, nag you old bag
Brag in the evening, my thingies don't sag
Snag in the covers, I'm left with no rag
Mag you're a menace, get rid of that fag!

Dusky Desire

Saba I. Khan
Jeddah, Saudi Arabia

This compassionate vibe, blushful wind
Sees solitary lurking moon, a lonely night
Dismiss not my desire, declined
Reminisce memories of our love's plight...

My eternal hopes of being loved again
Defy this lusty soul to replenish, rather insolent
Lie and wither away down the lane
Thy true heart, free me I pray, from this forlorn imprisonment

This shimmering moist eyes of mine
Cease to please the lingering that dwells in the heart
He's my God for he makes my life divine
Ease this callous creature to have another blissful start

In no time, another night shall touch its harbor and
Begin to kiss the fresh morning glow, shield me like armor
Therein lies a thirsty desire to feel my lover
Spin this amorousness into a thick arbor...

ECCENTRICITY

Richard Wagnell
Montreal, Canada

Binge on what you've never tasted
Fringe benefits befit the magnificent
Unhinge because of chances wasted
Cringe before the heaven-sent

Muster all you can; it's dangerous
Cluster bombs are half the quotient
Bluster cast aside, you're cancerous
Luster restored through a fraudulent potion

Ectoplasm jury to a crime never incited
Phantasm touches and angelic induction
Orgasm once started yet never ignited
Spasm into nothing, a void of selfish suction

Eclectic or perhaps misunderstood
Hectic placement of a mind so eccentric
Forensic science never could
Predict somebody quite so electric.

Endeavour I!

Keith Metcalfe Drew
Beverley, East Yorkshire, United Kingdom

Engrained in my mind the lesson learned,
Remained in my heart all the love lost,
Enflamed the memories deep within,
Ashamed am I your heart I crossed,

Forever in this life to be alone,
Together we could ever be as one,
Tethered is my heart to ever mourn,
Endeavour I to ever right this wrong!

Exodus

Denis Nguyen,
Calgary, Alberta, Canada

Depravation did consume this broken land
Condemnation followed sending them into exile
Liberation came to free them from Egypt's hand
Regeneration came to heal what evil did defile

Light shone brilliantly within their darkness
Might rescued them when they made their plight
Night was broken revealing Glorious Brightness
Sight was restored bringing new hope and delight

Exploding Silence

Tiphanie Cole
Murfreesboro, Tennessee, USA

Know that we are not the same
Slow thought breathes in you
No words from you are forthcoming
Grow decay in your fermented thoughts glue

See yourself in this deep disgust I display
Angry expressions of impotent rage held within
Boundary that holds your tongue forever comatose
Purgatory of a hell had with unspoken indecision

Fairy Charm

Gaylene Lesser
Victoria, Australia

Meet the fairies in the dell
Treat yourself to magic's gift
Feet will dance their special spell
Beat in tune, away you'll drift

Sparks will fly throughout the night
Arcs of stars will bless your time
Marks of wonder taking flight
Larks of fairy dance sublime

Fantasy World

Lori Gagnon
Anoka, Minnesota, USA

Understand imagination
Command fairies, they come alive
Expanding many elves entranced
Standing mystic worlds often thrive

Combine wizards their magic spells
Design leprechauns, dragons too
Assign mermaids they do exist
Align fantasy in your view

Fate's Hand

Olivia Annette Gates
Griffith, Indiana, USA

Abate all fears and calm thy being
Hate is not the way to go,
Fate has a hand though you be not seeing.
Await the love that was lost long ago.

Time will pass, memories fade
Climb to eternity, see glory above,
I'm sure the future will serenade
Sublime characters searching for love...

Gallow Man's Invocation

Misty L. Bowers
Utah, USA

Shadow of an endless ocean,
Hollow in my heart's emotion,
Fallow in my soul's devotion,
Window is my poem's expression...

Below the surface endless motion,
Merlot my glass of meditation,
Tallow burns up my confession,
Crow to feed on my redemption...

Glacial Fault

Michael Austin
Worcestershire, United Kingdom

Green lichen covered rock face exposed,
Clean water cascades through glacial fault,
Serene, emptying itself gloriously,
Scene of a lagoon formed vault!

Lush fauna fantastically framing,
Hush this prehistoric majesty,
Blush that man shall abuse it,
Crush this too common travesty!

Grande Dame, Aphrodite, Beauty's Art

Gregg Rowe
Montreal, Canada

She swims amongst dolphins and flies with doves,
Trees of lime and apples amongst she strolls.
Be still my heart that's fluttering with love
Sea waves ~ foam arisen ~ upon she rolls.

Her tongue is snake sharp, her temper is quick
Myrrh scents of her skin fragrance tease my nose.
Cur kin absent from her soul, I'm a Mick
Ter River we sit reciting her prose.

Warms she his bed, Ares, the god of war
Storms her marriage with outside affairs.
Forms the battle starting the Trojan war,
Swarms psyche over beauty ~ her darest flare.

And yet with all these faults she still remains,
Hand in hand into men's fluttering hearts.
Plan to continue to walk in beauty my dame ~
Grande dame, Aphrodite, beauty's art!

Hart Island

Connie Chiechi
Sacramento, California, USA

Lost and homeless, their lives are gone.
Crossed off list, each a nameless soul.
Tossed in trench on New York island.
Cost to get there a paltry toll.

Despair consumed their final years.
Where they'll be buried friends won't know.
Unfair, their graves will be unmarked
there on Hart Island where they'll go.

Haunting Memories

Lady Dragonwyck
Texas, USA

Golden sunlight filters radiantly
Molten memories forever emblazon
Frozen in time and loves rapture
Explosion of sweet by-gone loves dawn

Breeze gently caresses my face
Tease my eyes closed in thought
Ease tension from my Life
Release sad memories of battles fought

He Freely Gave

Pamela H.
Jacksonville, Florida, USA

Above the city on a tiny hill,
Love was nailed to a wooden cross.
Of His own choice, He had free will.
Dove of God died for the lost.

He paid the debt I should have paid.
Free am I to make the choice.
The empty tomb where He was laid,
Be now filled with lifted voice.

Heartfelt Cry

Scott Venus
Melbourne, Australia

Confess, unto me the reasons why you act so cold
Address, every memory that causes me pain
Caress, my heart with the courage to move on
Distress, fills my mind as I witness love wane

Casual, the way in which you said goodbye
Manual, to your desires I wished I possessed
Gradual, your progression to dismiss my advances
Sensual, a feeling that's now very much suppressed

I'll See You Again

(In memory of Adam Boehling)
10.11.1986 – 27.04.2005

Gary Boehling
North Carolina, USA

Delays in memory of days gone by,
Rays with vision of a past sons cry.
Gaze into a soul that flies...so high
Praise this last cherished goodbye.

I remember his final words to me,
My son whispered "I love you pop"
Dry those tears, don't let one drop,
Rely on your faith, never let it stop.

Icarus

Paul Yardley
Perth, Australia

Wanting to fly up towards the sun
Flying forever higher into the sky
Passing the clouds he makes a run
Loosing inhibitions watch him fly

Breaking his way past atmosphere
Reaching up enchants his curiosity
Speeding through the stratosphere
Breaching the sun's heated ferocity

Dismay as he forgets the words
Stay close to the Earth my son
Display your affinity with birds
Play on the winds enjoy the fun

Melting wax disturbs his flight
Warning rings within his ears
Falling back gravity he fights
Exacerbating all of Icarus' fears

Intertwined

Bonita (Rivas) Johnson
Sumter, South Carolina, USA

Collections of old photographs of you
reflections of a better time and place
affections were all we gave each other
recollections now recall your face.

Although, my memories blur with time,
know you will live forever in my mind
though you are no longer here thoughts of you
flow freely, our souls still intertwined.

It's All About Choices

Marilyn D. F. Boire
Idyllwild, California, USA

Reflect on what is holy
Reject whatever's not
Correct all that's lowly
Select positive thought

Direct a route to take
Protect against the past
Detect what is at stake
Connect to gains that last

La Vita

Mario de Paz
Genoa, Italy

Pensieri, rivolti verso il mondo.
Sentieri, percorsi con fatica.
Quartieri, vissuti fino in fondo.
Voleri, espressi da un'amica.

La vita, che scorre troppo in fretta.
Addita la strada da seguire
Ambita, la donna che è perfetta.
Finita, allora puoi morire.

Last Goodbye

Giddy Nielsen-Sweep
Brisbane, Australia

Lying on this bed I hear the taps
Trying to detect when footfall stepped
Buying time until I hear soft raps
Dying takes its time I must accept

Please keep me strong, Lord when his tears cascade
Freeze time that I may kiss his lips again
Seize one more touch, just one more contact made
He's sacrificing much to ease my pain

Feeling warmest breath upon my cheek
Healing can't be owned by lowly souls
Kneeling by my bed I hear him seek
Pealing bells are chiming, the Bell tolls

Then one more flutter of the eyelash sees
When clear his face appears I know he's there
Ten cherubim ignore his saddest pleas
Heav'n keeps a special place with loving care.

Lento Audition (Cross Lento)

Mike Howes aka Silent Cougar
Dunragit, Scotland

Last in the door; I try hard to be cool,
Cast aside quickly, by all in the room,
Passed a full glass, so I don't look a fool,
Fast to accept, quickly drowning the gloom.

Cool to the throat; I drank it down real fast,
room for another, the bottle was passed,
fool that I am, I spoke up to the cast,
gloom dissipated, accepted at last.

Before all went quiet, I cracked a joke,
anymore whisky and I may get drunk,
hardcore I was not, so added some coke,
encore was shouted, as one more was sunk.

Joke taken well, I pulled of the encore,
drunk up one more glass, so I looked hardcore,
coke was not added, don't need anymore,
sunk like a pro, as I had done before.

Lento in Music Means Slow Down

Brenna Powers
La Crosse, Wisconsin, USA

Slow and peaceful, waiting for the time,
Though your energy excites your song,
Go meandering through fields of rhyme;
Show me how to make the journey long.

Slake your thirst with slow and careful draughts.
Make hot chocolate to warm your soul;
Shake off hurry; let yourself relax.
Take your time and resonate the whole.

Light of Love

Neshni Naidoo
Cape Town, South Africa

Go forth, step out into the world
Aglow with the light of love
Sow seeds of hope in every heart
Grow faith in the Lord above

Measure your life in units of love
Treasure each moment you've got
Pleasure gained in giving, forgiving
Leisure spent helping those we forgot

Long Players

Sally Carter
St Austell, Cornwall, United Kingdom

Dolcissimo we'll play our love again,
though lately passion's somewhat more risque.
Go gently, sweet, my back won't take the strain.
No, honestly, it feels just fine that way.

More haste, less speed, with your arthritic knee.
Poor dear, perhaps a stick is overdue,
before it seizes up too painfully.
Or let us rest; I'll lie and dream with you,

hold your dear cheek against my once-young face,
mould that familiar body tight to mine.
Enfold me in the strength of your embrace;
old love glows warm and rich as vintage wine.

Will you still cuddle close beside me when
chill winds foretell the dimming of our days?
Still you will be my man above all men.
'Til then my love is yours - all yours, always.

Look Within

Sindhura Radhakrishnan
Bangalore, India

Gold sun peeks out and thus my day begins,
Rolled out of bed, though I would love to stay,
Cold water splashed on, lest my slumber wins
Untold, unheard, my dreams I hold at bay.

So much to do, I'm not sure where to start,
"Go on", I say silently in my mind,
Although it's tough, I'd like to think I'm smart,
Slow and steady, my feet I slowly find.

Two kids, cooking and coding quite quickly,
Few things of all that's part of my each day,
Through soiled nappies and school books I can see,
True pigments of life's amazing array.

We make so much of all we need to do,
Decree the deed is tough before we try
See not what is, but what we just want to,
Esprit dampened, we shake our heads and sigh.

I realise my morns are not so bad,
My God, there's so much more that I can do,
Why did I balk, why did life make me sad?
By now my rants buried, I start anew.

Beware, my friend, take note of what I say,
There are times when you are your greatest foe,
Where there's a will, there's bound to be a way
Dare to find within you, your own hero...

Lost the Way

Sydney Ward
Bend, Oregon, USA

Burned my fingers with a delicate touch,
Yearned to be on the other side.
Learned the value of innocence,
Earned the guilt that decays me inside.

Lost my way on the path once again,
Frost overtook as I sat in the night.
Cost was much greater than I predicted,
Tossed up my sword, surrendered the fight.

Defeat consumed every human remain,
Sheet after sheet of paper to turn.
Neat as could be, the chapter was written,
Beat the idea now, don't let me return.

Hold me tightly, and steady my stand,
Fold the page over, forget the ordeal.
Mold me into who I'm supposed to have been.
Cold turns to warm, and scars left to heal.

Manic Musings

Susan Elizabeth Eckenrode
Ohio, USA

Twirling thoughts that won't be caught
whirl and dance inside my brain.
Swirling verses never wrought
curl into a strange refrain.

Seams I've ripped and then re-sewn,
schemes of things I've yet to do,
dreams of all the loves I've known
stream their rhymes the whole night through.

Masquerade

Steve Herbert
Whangarei, New Zealand

Now the memories come teeming,
How you left this poor boy dreaming.
Avow no more your words redeeming;
Allow my heart this golden gleaming.

Flights of fancy make me shiver;
Nights of passion by the river.
Rites of passage you'd deliver;
Delights of expert pleasure-giver.

Yearning for those times together,
Returning kisses soft as feather,
Learning how love's silken tether,
Turning cruelly, bites like leather.

Cursed these fancies all-pervading.
Burst besotted thoughts parading;
Thirst no more, let them go fading;
First love's merely masquerading.

Me, Myself and I

Zahra Abdul Adhim
Manama, Bahrain

Clean floats my abstract existence
serene, an enveloping canopy of clouds it abides
unseen my body and I lay, conspiring
between scenery below my heaviness resides

Author of life, myself below teaches me
ardor is where I aspire to be, however
bitter are both compared to where I stand
Yonder I shred chocolate fractures of memories forever

Mother

Qiang (Cathy) Yuen
Shanghai, China

She looked pretty in her floral cheongsam
Crispy morning gaze into father's eyes
~ He left for school, his routine program
We stared at the world beyond the sunrise.

One day the wind blew, blue of winter's overstaying
Pathway empty, with footprints unseen
Midway flowed tears when days saw nothing
Today, fifty years, in fields of green.

Soon lines crawled upon her soft velvet face
Strewn jú huā petals, children playing in pathways
Hewn logs weathered in place
Moon still searching for sun in the maze.

Pots on fire, teas boiling through the day
Dots yet to be joined, knots loosened
Spots to clear from memory, erase dismay
Tots all grown, unmindful, unburdened.

Move Forward

Jeremiah Lawrence
Indiana, USA

Moving forward and learning always through time
Choosing this form for a time as the divine
Using this form to say it show it and write more
Doing well you, to the absolute end last line

Negate all that you felt you knew to be true
Skate right on over wiser and older
Desecrate nothing decent good or noble
Debate nothing squabble not a cold shoulder

Practice this form for fun to be true
Exactest as you can to see what you be
Apparatus befitting of a writers need
Fastest to do all you can learning to see

Rock it out rip it up through and through
Chalk out the outline effort you place to see
Clock watching twiddling thumbs do not try
Stock your mind of other ways to see to be free

Learn all that you can every form to write
Churn out sparks of worthwhile inspiration
Burn the midnight oil until mornings light
Yearn to produce something for civilization

Advance forward always you will gain in time
Chance your luck push skill use effort and try
Dance with your yourself your writings words
Enhance yourself and your world by and by

My First Lento

Jack Ellison
Toronto, Ontario, Canada

Well here's my first attempt at a Lento
Tell me how am I doing so far?
Swell that you thought of including me
Hell I could be your next Lento star!

Send me a challenge and I get right on it
Tend to get all excited when I write
Lend me your ears and I'll do my best
End up with my ego taking flight

***

Lento Number Two

Jack Ellison
Toronto, Ontario, Canada

Here's number two, so how did I do
Clear I've mastered this clever form
Fear others might give up in frustration
Mere handfuls will weather the storm

Stay with it, you'll find it very interesting
Lay there Lento-ing through the night
Pray you don't wind up in the looney bin
Stay with it, and you'll soon get it right

NATURE

Jayashree T. Rao
Karnataka, India

Nature, splendid and mystique,
Features lofty hills and river
Creatures all splendid and unique
Treasures, each day fewer.

Birds of many kinds distinctly fly,
Herds of animals stray the jungle,
Weird noises and cry
Concurred by man, single.

Needling Life

Alfred Vassallo
Colchester, England, United Kingdom

My humble melody dies and is amiss,
Glorify the master of my demise,
Goodbye I am falling down in an abyss;
Testify that I'm not mentally wise.

Surely I shall not cry when I'll be dead
Poorly I shall turn myself into a blissful thing
Prematurely I will laugh viciously instead,
Obscurely though I know I was born needling.

Night Sweat

Tarringo T. Vaughan
South Windsor, Connecticut, USA

Diluted images collapsing in my mind/
polluted faces dancing all around.
Commuted thoughts whisper all this combined
recruited translations swirling in sound;

reaching for answers, I clench through my sleep
bleaching shadows that collide soaked and wet.
Screeching distortions shatter all that weep/teaching the
madness drenched in my night sweat

Night Water

Suelynn Parker
Mississippi, USA

Wrinkled canvas which soothes a sailor
Crinkled quietly for those drifting by,
Sprinkled and dashed by an astrologer's dream,
Twinkled the reflected eyes of the sky so nigh.

So dark is its face blend in the horizon,
Crows a deep tune from the spirits at sea,
Aglow floats a lamp by a ship forgotten,
Though the last glint of fin flicks with glee.

Noah's Search

Robert Lust
Boynton Beach, Florida, USA

You want me, Lord, to build a boat
To make it hold a zoo
Two of each animal I must find
Whew, that's a lot to do.

Bears I should find easily
Hares always live among us
There's going to be a problem, Lord
Where's the elusive platypus.

Of Spiders and Spring

B. Hopkins
West Midlands, United Kingdom

Blue Spiders

Do not place tiny spiders in your fridge
you know they'll get too cold and slowly die;
through culinary skill I've come to know
blue spiders don't taste nice in apple pie.

So let them sleep in peace under your bed,
no icy graves for them, it's just not done;
though, careful in the morning where you tread
go slowly, lest you tear the webs they've spun.

Spring

May springtime birth with buds of gentle blue;
away these hues of winter's dullish grain
dismay has walked beside me winter through
stay with me not, give up your bitter reign.

Sweet rose your fragrance haunts me as I wait
greet now my prayers with petals 'neath the sun;
deceit is all that winter can create
retreat I say, depart, your worst is done.

Oh No... A Lento

Rodger Moyer
Harleysville, Pennsylvania, USA

Hooray! the day is finally here!
Display or pay the price
Daresay the Lento piqued my fear
Entree to this advice;

Extend each man your willing hand
Defend a friend in need
Ascend from fates of shifting sand
Transcend a world of greed

Withstand each year of pain and tears
Demand and stand for truth
Command your heart through all your fears
Expand beyond your youth

Try every door, seek and explore
Fly in the sky you choose
Cry for the souls who are no more
Goodbyes will bring the "blues"

Show every child they have a style
Sow seeds to feed their souls
Bestow the wisdom of your miles
Go forth as life unfolds

Give every goal your heart and soul
Forgive transgressions past
Outlive the strife that seeks control
Live each day as your last

On Strike!

Gllen Pappaachan
Malappuram, Kerala, India

Blocking roads, they create a chaos,
Holding red flags they shout,
Striking seems to be their birth right.
Numbering in hundreds, they're out.

Showing their strength is their weapon,
Chanting a slogan is their norm,
Mocking the government, their style,
Striking today is totally out of form.

Putting life of common man in jeopardy,
Wiping tears of the oppressed is their mantra
Breaking rules for them is but a game,
Shouting against the government, a tantra.

Boiling deep inside me, is my anger,
Failing to comprehend their reason,
Creating unrest is the only way they know?
Striking ~ another unbearable season.

One Might Ask

Michael John McCrae
New Jersey, USA

though wondering about life's trials
show sadly, insecurity's thrust
grow doubtful thoughts to saving faith
throw to cold winds salvation's trust

there might be need to ask the question
share with a soul what life had lent
bare last his portion, wisdom's goals
where one should fold his final tent

OUT-OF-STATE CASH

Lawrence Eberhart
Sparks, Nevada, USA

I ask cashiers "Do you accept out of state cash?"
Try this on folks with spiels they must have to rehearse.
Why you'll find many will think you've asked something rash,
Buy time seeming to search and fumble through your purse.

Few youngsters will answer without a call for aid.
True, some will ask you what you mean, but others call
to managers, with this new puzzle you've portrayed.
You simply pay with cash minted elsewhere, that's all.

Outcast

Jill Pennell
Northfleet, Gravesend, Kent, England

Staying together a big mistake
Saying those things you hurt me so
Playing happy families hiding the truth
Weighing the possibilities you had to go

Your family to them I'm an outcast
More lonely I have become each day
Before I had a life with many friends
Sure you made them stay away

Perfect Rain Dance

Kashinath Karmakar (Kash Poet)
Durgapur, India

Cold rain drops on your face
Boldly touch your lips with bliss,
Hold my hand, let's do a rain dance,
Old memories ignite our first kiss.

Get closer to my mouth dear
Let our breaths mingle once
Set the stage for a perfect kiss
Bet this is our best rain dance.

Prayer's Conversation

Reason A. Poteet
New Albany, Indiana, USA

Crying out to God with problems to face,
vying with sleep, my thinking's a chore.
Buying back time while seeking His grace,
trying to pray sounds more like a snore,

How to decide the time that one prays -
vow to start praying ere time is spent,
bow recognizing distress in life's maze.
Thou, Father God - my empowerment!

Releasing my prayers all through the day,
decreasing the chance of evil inspiration,
policing my actions, God's will to convey,
unceasing prods of prayer's conversation.

Ablaze with light, each new moment is born.
Praise for God's strength after trust's rebirth;
malaise withdraws in the wake of its scorn.
Thruways of prayer help me cope on earth.

PRELUDE

Joao Camilo de Oliveira Torres,
Belo Horizonte, Minas Gerais, Brazil

Loving thee is like loving time;
embracing blindly elusive shadows;
sealing daily a vow sublime;
dancing wildly as liberty endows.

Promises are graved in marble;
muses are sculpted by my dreams;
senses are purified of all garble
roses bud ageless as moonbeams...

Princess Shahrzad (Acrostic Lento)
(Written for Shahrzad Maftooh)

Jim T. Henriksen
Norway, Scandinavia

Showing all that she's a princess,
Holding readers with her rhymes,
Amazing with words like flowers,
Hinting us to ancient times...

Reading all the words of her friends,
Zapping with her sharp critique,
Adoring in her sweet comments,
Drawing new friends with technique.

PROMISES

Sharon Cawthorne
Sheffield, Yorkshire, England,

Behind a golden mask of dreams
Unwind within a timeless sea.
Find the key to a world supreme
Entwined in perfect harmony.

Believe in faith, embrace it tight
Leave this sleep, wake and rise.
Breathe and suckle a new born light
Reave the wonders before one's eyes.

Reality

Akinwunmi Elijah
Ogun State, Nigeria

Desire, as ever, will always ignite the flames,
Fire, with zeal, will make morn of night;
Dire needs are the bereavements of the heart,
Aspire not, if for their real sights you cannot fight.

Set upon the waters the fires of passion,
Let their heats be cooled with no end;
Whet your thirst when their powers are dying, lest
Regret become your eternal friend.

Requiem for an Abused Child

Larry A. Tilander
Belleville, Ontario, Canada

Born to cruelty, no chance.
Scorn; her fate, a peasant lass.
Torn and broken by the road.
Mourn this innocent and pass.

Now you cry with outraged voice
"How", you ask "comes this to be?"
Vow to me to stop abuse.
Allow no more this destiny.

She Poet

Khara Elizabeth House
Flagstaff, Arizona, USA

When I was just a little girl
Often I would sit and wonder why
Men seemed to get the glory of the
Pen with words that made the women cry.

Inside I knew that I could be the
Pride of every poet's glistening
Eye if, even as softer sexed, I
Tried to keep the whole world listening.

Simply Love

Anna Martha Klimstra
Broeksterwâld, Friesland, The Netherlands

Fly through the sky
Deny you're up high
Espy with your eye
Reply with a sigh

Stay on the ground
Play with your hound
Sway by each sound
Today love is found

Six Phone Calls Since We Talked

Laurie Kolp
Southeast, Texas, USA

and I feel like pickled beets, my
hand is shaking the phone as I
brand politicians pesky flies
stand beneath their shallow lies.

Yes?" I say because I know
less than this restricted foe
guess the motive, much too slow,
gets lots of hang-ups on Joe Blow

like I've done two times before.
Psyched to stop this raging war
spike the line, even the score
strike deceit with wild boars,

I plan to march in Washington
cry, "Harassment, everyone!
Why bother me with voices spun?"
Sigh~ then you called, and I was done.

Sitting Here

Olwin McDonald,
Belfast, Northern Ireland

Sitting here, watching the world go by.
Hitting this bottle again tonight.
Sipping its venom, till it runs dry.
Belittling this poison and its plight.

Numb, my heart hears church bells chime.
Come they say, and you will see.
Some inner voice say's "It is time...
Succumb, and let me satisfy thee."

Socialization

Stucz Arnold
Satu Mare, Romania

Trouble is we don't visualize
Grumble for days and no sweet talk
A stumble, now can't realize
Bubble inside ~ stuck, can't walk.

Gainless gadgets and fancy phones
Senseless living, no hugs, no kisses
Faithless people with no backbones
Happiness, love and care she wishes.

Those long and lonely nights
Whose priority is being online
Goes through all life's fights
Knows none why so close is the skyline.

Becoming so cold and very selfish
Working hard just for some money
Feeling a sting like that of a jellyfish
Praying just to taste again the honey.

Fish can't change the ocean all alone
Wish we had no fences, no borders
Dish not good enough, nor sweet is a melon
Leash around neck following others orders.

Simply raw times we are going through
Cruelty in our heart is growing
Serenity is slowly fading too
Finally dying alive without even knowing.

Some Drink (Some Shouldn't)

Valerie Jean Schafer
Plymouth, Indiana, USA

Some people get solace from a bottle of gin,
Rum relieves the pain better for others.
Dumb is the man, who thinks he can win,
Come will the devil from the bottle he smothers.

Drink if you dare, but if you choose to,
Think about it long, hard and well.
Wink at the devil that lies within you,
Sink not by choice, into the misery of hell.

Spring Caprice

Jeremy Martin
Keene, New Hampshire, USA

Dawn shall begin to stir beneath the trees
Yawn slow and long, the forest still sleep
Drawn up to kiss the violets all with ease
Faun calls through pipes and walks on hilltops steep

Beneath the canopy that filters sun
Bequeath, young satyr, all your melodies
Unsheathe the sticks and flowers, spring's begun
Wreath moon with stars and winter's memories

Stream of Consciousness

Sharon Anderson
New York, USA

Go now to dreams and seek your lines.
No consequences linger there.
Slow rhythms waltz in fine designs;
show you the way, if you but dare.

In free flow, verses swirl and wind.
Within; the threads that weave your song.
Yin and Yang are there to find.
Begin. It's been there all along.

Sweet Baby Boy

Jenna Caniglia-Graves
Bellevue, Nebraska, USA

Peeking into your cozy crib,
Seeking your heart melting smile.
Speaking of bottles, binky, and bib.
Sneaking some snuggles awhile.

Giggly moments alone with you.
Wiggly little fingers and toes.
Jiggly belly pudgy and new.
Wriggly baby just grows and grows.

Pleasing you with some peek-a-boo.
Squeezing in a nursery rhyme.
Teasing you with a tickle or two.
Seizing this moment in time.

Beaming at you with parent's pride.
Dreaming of all you can be.
Gleaming eyes that hold smiles inside,
Seeming to love all you see.

Bringing you in close to my chest.
Singing a light happy tune.
Stringing together words you love best.
Clinging to this fine afternoon.

Playing beside my dear little boy,
Staying near your sweet baby smell.
Paying mind to what brings you joy.
Praying that life treats you well.

The Day You Left

Lydia Woronchak
La Prairie, Canada

Do you remember when you went away?
Who could forget a painful thing like that?
You didn't look back, or decide to stay
Two hours later, dad thought he 'smelled a rat'.

When he came home, and found out you had left
Again and again, he questioned, "Why, Oh why?"
Then he was hurt, and felt extreme bereft
Men like him can get so angry they can die.

I know now it was what you had to do
Why did you have to go and leave me so?
My young heart nearly broke in two
By the time I realized you'd let me go.

We all took the fall for you that day
He told us never to speak to you again
"She" was no longer a word that we could say
Be it as it may, we knew no better then.

Although it happened so many years ago
So many times I've run it through my mind
Though I have had a lot of time to grow
No one can fully leave the past behind.

Someday I hope I truly will forget
Away I'll place this memory for all time
Someway I Know I'll live without regret
Today has already been a longtime.

The Lone Ranger

Late Robert Edgar Burns
New Port Richey, Florida, USA

Departing on his white stallion,
Starting his patrol was heard to say,
Carting along his sidekick Tonto while
Parting, "Hi-yo, Silver! Away!"

Named by Tonto "Kemosahbee,"
Famed silver bullets were his tools.
Framed in pictures riding his horse Silver.
Shamed the bad guys who looked like fools!

The Love Rippled

Yanny Widjanarko
Surabaya, Indonesia

Don't wake me from this dream, if this is a dream
Throne at last, as we celebrate life after the scar
Alone in my sanity, this noise drives me crazy
Drone of the dark life has sunk me too far

Let me dwell safely in your arms
Set me free from bondage of the tangled chain
Vignette of this might be fragile or blur
Yet it's the survival beneath the pouring rain

This Night

Heather Hazlett
Waxhaw, North Carolina, USA

Away from the world
Stay with me tonight
Lay down beside me
Play under the stars' light

Give into our desire
Live for you and I
Captive in your gaze
Relive this moment in time

Time Soothes

Doris Culverhouse
Georgia, USA

Accuse my heart of desire and then frigidity
Abuse my senses and feelings for minor infractions
Refuse my affections and my friendly kindness
Defuse this plan I have in my minds repetitions

Favor my green eyes charming glances again
Savor my gentle touches, caress this heart again, remove the wedges.
Hey your days are numbered prophesies your lying tongue
Say more and more, desires dwindle, time smoothes the edges

Too Quickly Passes Spring

Sharon Miller Bolander
Flushing, Michigan, USA

Epitomized is springtime's dream
Mesmerized by satin breeze
Characterized renewing theme
Idolized through winter's freeze.

Sought to capture its perfume
Bought by those who long for youth
Caught inside a budding bloom,
Fraught is age in fleeting truth.

Triple Lento I e II

M. Herrera
Edmonton, Canada

I touch her silence with my silence:
Sigh and you will have touched my hand;
cry and you will have touched my absence.
Lie to me that everything is grand.

Kiss me, taste me with your tender lips.
Miss me? Darling, you, I surely miss!
Bliss, My Love, has sank like many ships.
This is now a year gone by, amiss.

I touch her quiet skin as soft as foam;
sigh, I do, for her mystic river smile;
cry, sometimes, I cry, for she is home.
Fly? I cannot leave her, not a while.

Let me touch your silence one more time
(yet once more is not nearly enough).
Wet are my eyes for Death must be a crime
set to haunt us, darling, long and rough.

If they only knew how sweet her face
~ grief is sad companionship for her.
Thief: this death that took me without grace!
Brief, my time, yet lasting, love and her.

I touch her silence with my silence:
Sigh and you will have touched my hand;
cry and you will have touched my absence.
Lie to me that everything is grand!

Veto Power

Dabir Ahmed
Mumbai, India

Modesty, honesty, spirit, sacrifice,
Creativity swallowed dreadful wolf,
Dreadfully wild untamed greed,
Certainly piled up weapons, deadlier wolf.

Tall Peace talks in halls packed,
Stall resolutions tabled and lost
Call veto power eclipses moon of hope ever,
Wall truth goodness beauty ever rocked.

We Deserve Better

Dis-illusioned
New York, USA

Dummies sign in Sequester;
tummies, to feel hunger pangs.
Yummies, off the register;
mommies bare survival fangs.

Law makers loaf on The Hill.
Raw fakers is what they are.
Paw shakers, making a kill;
jaw breakers, all playing czar.

Richest nation in the world--
greatest country on the earth.
A test now sees us unfurled;
latest one to lose its mirth.

We, the people, deserve more;
see the sweat and blood we've paid.
Be that Yankee who must soar,
free and brave, to never fade.

When Mr. Right Comes By

Agnes L. Kirby
Okotoks, Alberta, Canada

White rabbits in pink paisley coats -
bright visions I am seeing now.
Right love came by and smiled at me,
knight on bold steed changed drab to wow!

Why do I seem to walk on air?
Spry feet have wings and joy is mine.
I raise my glass, propose a toast,
my guy is utterly divine.

This is the way that angels feel,
bliss filled and blessed they shout and sing.
His hand in mine, him by my side,
is all I want, it's ev'rything!

Oh, welcome are love's wondrous sights...
so bring those furry bunnies on!
Go tell the world that I am sure,
no love before so gaily shone.

When Voters Speak

Kimberly Watson
Fairbanks, Alaska

Direction changes, this chaotic age;
Connection to charisma now estranged.
Election results turn prophetic page,
Rejection of unfulfilled hope and change.

Delusion burst, intrudes reality;
Confusion not dispelled without a fee.
Infusion of ideas bring unity,
Conclusion; there's a cost to being free.

Whereas, Camelot's pristine walls crumble,
Has cost inflated all beyond repair?
Jazz man's tune extols our blues in tumble,
as diagnosis pass to new health care.

Stand together, speak bold with single voice,
Band red, white, and blue; bound by common goal.
Strand of hope dangles with freedom of choice,
Brand us Americans and make us whole.

WHITE ROSES FOR HIROSHIMA

Shubham Sharma
Udhampur, Jammu & Kashmir, India

Smoky cloud over angry ashes, skinning
tiny lives, lifeless under satiated sky
inhumanity killing humanity, how ironic!
rivalry of nations unmindful of small fry.

Effortless effort to revive withered flowers,
Countless cries of falling feather,
Helpless kin, rising from despair,
Sadness concealed in stench of leather.

Tyrant epoch: A horror, now and tomorrow
Potent darkness ~ A curse to that day,
Silent victims of experiment and wrath,
Dormant emotions died with folks they slay.

Smitten by pangs of sorrowed souls
Sadden mine yet brings hope with its cease,
Laden with tears for my departed dears,
Shrunken God! Lay now their souls in peace!

Wyoming

Jack Huber
Denver, Colorado, USA

Dwell on Wyoming, its soft, clouded sky,
smell the plains' air as the fragrances drift,
tell us of eagles in early July,
quell nature's passion before spirits lift.

Nights in the open are filled with such stars,
rites of the passage of earth and of man,
sites where a clan had drawn circles and bars,
whites and dull reds in a Yellowstone tan.

Author's Note

I truly admire the work of Liang Zong for artfully presenting the Lento in combined forms. Skillfully offering to the senses, one can discover where the poetess comes from. Luck, a belief that came down from generations, seemingly is changing with the modern generation. I can't begin to explain how much I love the opening of this poem, as if she is preparing the reader or welcoming with incense, creating that fragrance of Yulan, then revealing that deep message through the Lento and similarly giving a fading effect at the end.

Yellow River – Combined Forms

Liang Zhong
Guangzhou, Guangdong, China

Fragrance of Yulan
Mystical, magical
Like a surge of dreams
Swallowing your entire being
Believing, disbelieving
Overwhelmed,
awaiting...

Luck is the promise of the eastern wind
Lilac dreams of women with virgin womb
Ducks shan't swim in the yellow river for fear of being
Struck by destiny to their doom.

Luck is the promise of the eastern wind
Havoc in the heart, hassle in the head,
Hillocks bare from wrath of the rain
Stuck with hope, and faith that's long fled...

Fragrance of Yulan
fades,
seasons change
The yellow river of luck
flows...
flows...
flows...

Author's Note

The 101st Lento is the story of my parents against the stories of thousands of couples in the world. I feel in the era they got married; life was much simpler, yet offered an abundance of happiness. I am the result of this happiness, which teaches me, no matter in which time span I am traveling, the heart is the same: the heart, that machinery which induces your whole being and generates love. There's so little tolerance in our world today, and matters seem easier being spoken than lived, but glorious are those who weathered the storms and like John the Baptist said, the rest of us are not worthy to untie their laces. So sacred is love and those who live in love. This Cross Lento is a tribute to my parents celebrating their fifty years of marriage squabbling and bearing four children and for those millions of couples who "happily quarrel ever after". But then… in the words of my personal doctor, Virginia Brearley, "Marriage wouldn't be exciting without all those quarrels and fights, would it? I've been married for 13 years and my husband and I fuss about simple things as to who has to feed the cat!"

Love's Eternal Glitter
(Cross Lento)

If love was a splendored thing
Cliffs would see less pain beneath
Kerchiefs and handkerchiefs seeing
Different faces and a smile with it.

What is the world without affection?
~ frost forms faster, feud and frustration
Hot cakes soon turning to imperfection
Lost to find love, turn in another direction.

Happily lived ever after, many a folk
Bumpy or blessed mattered not the ride
Dearly cloaking even as they woke broke
Infidelity has now flown in with the tide.

Still, what is this world without devotion?
Body, a mere machine: just parts, no emotion
Thrill, brief as a flicker, willpower shrunken
Gaudy worldly desires, vain attraction.

Many yet, lived happily (or not) ever after,
Barely a word spoken to stir the mind
Empty rooms, life too, blind love growing blinder
Safety of separation seemed rather unkind.

And yet in love the world is constantly falling
Adore its pain unending, ravingly accepting
Stranded bliss, revering, sanctifying
For love is splendid, eternally glittering.

How to write Lento?

The Lento was invented in the winter of 2005 by Lencio Dominic Rodrigues. The form has no relation to music or the other similar sounding poetic form, Cento.

A Lento consists of a minimum of two quatrains with a **fixed** end rhyme scheme of abcb, defe. Rhyme enthusiasts however, may also rhyme the first and the third lines, although it is not a requirement. But, what sets the Lento apart is its **unique feature of monorhyme of the first word (or its syllable) of each line in the quatrain**. Hence a basic Lento would look like the following exhibit:

g ________________ a
g ________________ b
g ________________ c
g ________________ b
h ________________ d
h ________________ e
h ________________ f
h ________________ e

OR

g ________________ a
g ________________ b
g ________________ a
g ________________ b
h ________________ c
h ________________ d
h ________________ c
h ________________ d

An example of a basic Lento:

Royal Asylum

Dreams built, for many a seeker
Beams of hope revealed to them seeking peace
Seems like a country of contrasting culture
Streams of those taking Britain on lease!

Hail Queen of mercy, you say it's all fair
They'll escape jail for something simple as sex
Females may go about flaunting their hair
Wail sadly, poor civilians paying their tax!

Just as every form has rules, so does a Lento. One may want his poem to be longer than just eight lines and may build up four quatrains to make it a double Lento, or a six-versed to call it a triple Lento. Finally, a poem with more than seven verses is called a Lento chain.

Example of a double Lento:

Tears for the African Soil

Skinny shoulders and skulls, eyes like dry pebbles
Nearly on death's door, curvy as a winding road
Nudely, devoid even of wild grains and drizzles
Hungry and starved, span of life narrowed.

Green was once, the jungles with their beast
Sin of our hands brought drought upon our lands
Ravines roasted and cruel cracks on fields exist,
Clean wondrous wealth, now turned to wastelands.

True what they say, we reap what we sow
Due is what we get, mother earth hasn't slept yet
new warning always, but our noises only grow
Into our hands is our fate, my brothers, don't forget!

Fragile heart, eyes flowing tears heavy as pebbles
Little angels look like beast only heard of, not seen
Brittle bones building boundless ghostly jungles
Battle of a million lives, a battle we all wish to win.

A variation to make Lento more fun was introduced in 2012. Named as Cross Lento, the rhyme pattern alternates in the reverse as seen in the following exhibit. However, the opening verse will still remain the same as that of a basic Lento with the monorhyme at the beginning.

g ____________________ a
g ____________________ b
g ____________________ a or c
g ____________________ b
d ____________________ h
e ____________________ h
d or f ____________________ h
e ____________________ h
i ____________________ k
i ____________________ l
i ____________________ k or m
i ____________________ l
n ____________________ j
o ____________________ j
n or p ____________________ j
o ____________________ j

An example of a Cross Lento:

Plumeria Memories

Plumeria withers into the summer
Blooming now: old memories and
Broom flowers seemingly in splendor
Groom my heart, for a brand new hand.

Calm seemed the waters we sailed
Lies and lies got trains derailed
Balm never soothed hearts that ailed
Sighs too, did no good when exhaled.

Gold turns to dust, time spent, to waste
Cold, grows to new love: the hurting heart
Old, same old bitter taste
Holds inside your heart, hard to depart.

Returns plumeria with fragrance anew
More of fresh dew days and less to argue
Learns from past to easily bid adieu
Your doings will give you what you're due.

There's nothing mathematical about the Lento, no fixed syllable structure although a good meter is recommended. Many poets around the world find the Lento a fun way of penning down their thoughts. Others make it more interesting by applying various other tools of poetry. After all, isn't it what poetry is about?

Glossary

Bullocky ~ Australian term for the driver of a bullock team, the same as Bullwhacker in America who would drive an ox wagon or other heavy freight wagon especially in the early settlement of the West.

Cheongsam ~ a one-piece Chinese dress for women, also known as the mandarin gown.

Jú huā ~ Chrysanthemum flower used for making tea and herbal remedies.

Mick ~A disparaging term for a person of Irish descent.

Sassafras ~ A species of deciduous trees, native to eastern North America and eastern Asia, once extensively used as a fragrance in perfumes and soaps, food and for aromatherapy. Sassafras extract was a primary ingredient in root beer, until it was banned by FDA in 1960 for mass production. It has been discovered that that an oil produced by the sassafras trees called safrole was proven to be carcinogenic.

Tantra ~ A Ritual.

Ter ~ ***The Ter*** is a river in *Catalonia* (north eastern *Spain*) that begins in the mountains of the ***Pyrenees,*** passes through the city of ***Girona***, and ends in the ***Mediterranean Sea*** at ***l'Estartit***.

Yulan ~ Yulan Magnolia is native to central and eastern China and is commonly cultivated in Chinese Buddhist temple gardens. The flowers were regarded as a symbol of purity in the Tang Dynasty and were grown in the gardens of the Emperor's palace. It is the official city flower of Shanghai.